## SPORTS INJURIES:
## HOW TO PREVENT, DIAGNOSE, & TREAT

# BASKETBALL

# Sports Injuries:
# How to Prevent, Diagnose, & Treat

- Baseball
- Basketball
- Cheerleading
- Equestrian
- Extreme Sports
- Field
- Field Hockey
- Football
- Gymnastics
- Hockey
- Ice Skating
- Lacrosse
- Soccer
- Track
- Volleyball
- Weight Training
- Wrestling

## SPORTS INJURIES:
## HOW TO PREVENT, DIAGNOSE, & TREAT

# BASKETBALL

### JOHN WRIGHT

Severn River Middle
Media Center

MASON CREST PUBLISHERS
www.masoncrest.com

**Mason Crest Publishers Inc.**
**370 Reed Road**
**Broomall, PA 19008**
**(866) MCP-BOOK (toll free)**
**www.masoncrest.com**

First printing

1 2 3 4 5 6 7 8 9 10

Library of Congress Cataloging-in-Publication Data on file
at the Library of Congress

ISBN 1-59084-627-3

Series ISBN 1-59084-625-7

Editorial and design by
Amber Books Ltd.
Bradley's Close
74–77 White Lion Street
London N1 9PF
www.amberbooks.co.uk

**Project Editor**: Michael Spilling
**Design**: Graham Curd
**Picture Research**: Natasha Jones

Printed and bound in the Hashemite Kingdom of Jordan

**PICTURE CREDITS**
**Corbis**: 6, 8, 10, 11, 12, 15, 16, 18, 20, 21, 23, 25, 27, 28, 30, 32, 36, 39, 43, 46, 48, 50, 52, 53, 54, 55, 56, 59; ©**EMPICS**: 49.

**FRONT COVER**: All Corbis, except ©EMPICS (bl).

**ILLUSTRATIONS**: Courtesy of Amber Books except:
**Bright Star Publishing plc**: 40, 42, 45.

---

**IMPORTANT NOTICE**

This book is intended to provide general information about sports injuries, their prevention, and their treatment. The information contained herein is not intended as a substitute for professional medical care. Always consult a doctor before beginning any exercise program, and for diagnosis and treatment of any injury. Accordingly, the publisher cannot accept any responsibility for any prosecution or proceedings brought or instituted against any person or body as a result of the use or misuse of the techniques and information within.

# CONTENTS

Foreword 6

History 8

The Mental Game 18

Fitness to Avoid Injury 28

Injuries and Treatment 36

Careers in Basketball 50

Glossary 60

Further Information 62

Index 64

# Foreword

*Sports Injuries: How to Prevent, Diagnose, and Treat* is a seventeen-volume series written for young people who are interested in learning about various sports and how to participate in them safely. Each volume examines the history of the sport and the rules of play; it also acts as a guide for prevention and treatment of injuries, and includes instruction on stretching, warming up, and strength training, all of which can help players avoid the most common musculoskeletal injuries. *Sports Injuries* offers ways for readers to improve their performance and gain more enjoyment from playing sports, and young athletes will find these volumes informative and helpful in their pursuit of excellence.

Sports medicine professionals assigned to a sport that they are not familiar with can also benefit from this series. For example, a football athletic trainer may need to provide medical care for a local gymnastics meet. Although the emergency medical principles and action plan would remain the same, the athletic trainer could provide better care for the gymnasts after reading a simple overview of the principles of gymnastics in *Sports Injuries*.

Although these books offer an overview, they are not intended to be comprehensive in the recognition and management of sports injuries. The text helps the reader appreciate and gain awareness of the common injuries possible during participation in sports. Reference material and directed readings are provided for those who want to delve further into the subject.

Written in a direct and easily accessible style, *Sports Injuries* is an enjoyable series that will help young people learn about sports and sports medicine.

*Susan Saliba, Ph.D., National Athletic Trainers' Association Education Council*

Flying high off the court. A basketball net can be hung anywhere, from a garage door to an oak tree.

# History

**Basketball is the only team sport with mass appeal that was created in the United States. Our other favorite sports developed from English games: baseball from rounders, and football from soccer and rugby. But basketball was born in 1891 in Springfield, Massachusetts.**

Americans soon became aware that this is a fast, exciting game. It is simple, too, requiring only a basketball, two baskets, and five players per team. Indeed, it is so simple and so spectacular that more than 300 million people now play it worldwide.

The inventor of basketball was actually a Canadian who was teaching in the United States. James Naismith (1861–1939), a Presbyterian minister, was a physical education instructor at the YMCA's International Training School in Springfield. Asked to create an indoor game for bored students during the harsh New England winter, he first tried soccer and lacrosse in the gym. When these games injured players and broke windows, Naismith asked the school superintendent for two square boxes to nail at a height of 10 feet (3 m) at either end of the gym. However, only two half-bushel peach baskets were available in the storeroom, so these became the goals. For this reason, one of his students, Frank Mahan, suggested calling the game "basket ball." (Otherwise, we might be playing "boxball" to this day!) This first game on December 21, 1891, was between teams of nine players each because Naismith had eighteen students; the score was 1–0.

Lew Alcindor, later named Kareem Abdul-Jabbar, towers over UCLA Coach John Wooden as he holds his Most Valuable Player award when his team won the 1968 NCAA Championship.

Naismith wrote down thirteen rules for his new game, and when the students went home for their Christmas vacation, they introduced basketball to their local YMCAs, many of which were in Canada. The game spread rapidly: by 1892, two colleges were playing basketball—Geneva College in Beaver Falls, Pennsylvania, and the University of Iowa.

Two years later, the game had been introduced in England, France, Australia, India, and China. By then, American players had become tired of climbing ladders to retrieve the ball and had switched to using baskets with the bottoms cut out. In 1892, wire baskets appeared, and a year later wire backboards were in place (to keep spectators in the balcony from interfering with play). In 1904, to prevent players from bending the wire backboards to help funnel shots into their basket, which had been the practice, wooden backboards became mandatory. Four years later, these were replaced by glass backboards.

Early basketball teams would look strange to today's fans. Naismith's players wore wool jerseys

James Naismith, the father of basketball, displays the basic equipment for the game, including an example of the original basket, a peach basket with no opening at the bottom.

# WILT CHAMBERLAIN (1936–1999)

Remarkable player Wilt Chamberlain was inducted into the Naismith Basketball Hall of Fame in 1978.

Nicknamed "Wilt the Stilt" and the "Big Dipper," Wilt Chamberlain has been called the most awesome force ever seen on a basketball court. At 7 feet 1 inch (2.15 m) and 275 pounds (125 kg), he was unstoppable. He was the only NBA player to score 100 points in one game, and his other single-game records included eighteen straight field goals without a miss and fifty-five rebounds. He also held the NBA career record of 23,924 rebounds, was the second all-time scorer with 31,419 (behind Kareem Abdul-Jabbar), and was the only NBA player to score 4,000 points in one season.

Chamberlain played two years with the University of Kansas, and was named All-American both years. He then spent a season with the professional Harlem Globetrotters before becoming the NBA's Rookie of the Year in 1959 with the Philadelphia Warriors. In 1964, he joined the Philadelphia 76ers and was traded to the Los Angeles Lakers in 1968.

Retiring in 1973, Chamberlain had one other astonishing statistic: in 1,200 games, he never fouled out. He explained this with a smile: "They said I was too nice."

with long sleeves and long pants. Their only shot from the field was the two-handed set shot. If a player was fouled, anyone on the team could shoot the free throw. Teams had any number of players (fifty on each side at Cornell in 1892) until the number was fixed at five in 1895. The

original games were bruising affairs that often ended in fights. Wire cages were constructed around some courts not only to protect fans from the brawls, but also to keep the audience from hurling bottles and other items, including nails, onto the court. This is why basketball is still called the "cage game." Some referees even carried guns for crowd control. The YMCA banned basketball in the 1890s, so games often took place in unsuitable halls with stairways, offices, pillars, even posts in the middle of the

Many basketball games are won at the free-throw line. A player is able to take his time, with a clear view of the basket, but the pressure is intense.

court—which is why we talk about a "post play" when a player acts as a "screen" (blocker) for a teammate about to shoot.

The sport eventually became more civilized and began gaining popularity in high schools. One team in Passaic, New Jersey, was known as the "Wonder Team" when it won 159 straight games between 1919 and 1925. Basketball became an official Olympic sport at the 1936 games in Berlin. The growing college game was given its first national tournament in 1937 by the National Association of Intercollegiate Athletics (NAIA). This was followed by the National Invitational Tournament (NIT) in 1938 and the National Collegiate Athletic Association (NCAA) tournament a year later.

The sport was also a favorite with women. The first women's college game was in 1893 between the freshmen and sophomore classes at Smith College in Northampton, Massachusetts. An amateur team of Canadian women, the Edmonton Commercial Graduates ("Grads"), won 502 games from the 1920s through the 1940s against both women's and men's teams; this included 147 consecutive victories. The Women's National Basketball Association (WNBA) began play in 1997 and drew a record 2,362,430 fans during the 2002 season. By 2003, it had sixteen teams competing in its annual championship. The U.S. women's Olympic team won the gold medal in 1984, 1988, 1996, and 2000.

## BASKETBALL GOES PROFESSIONAL

Professional men's teams began to appear at the end of the nineteenth century. They included the Buffalo Germans; New York Wanderers; Kansas City Blue Diamonds; the New York Celtics, who had a 204–11 record in the 1922–1923 season; and the New York Renaissance (the "Rens"), an African-American team that once won 88 straight games. The entertaining Harlem Globetrotters began their first tour in 1926, went twenty-four years without losing, and in 1998 played their 20,000th game.

The first professional league was the National Basketball League (NBL), formed in 1898. It disbanded, and a new league with the same name was established in the Midwest in 1937. In 1946, the National Hockey League began the Basketball Association of America (BAA) to make greater use of their facilities. The two basketball leagues merged in 1949 to form the National Basketball Association (**NBA**), which had twenty-nine teams in 2003. Only three of the original eleven BAA teams remain in today's NBA: the Boston Celtics, New York Knickerbockers, and Philadelphia Warriors (who moved to San Francisco and are now the Golden State Warriors). Professional players first participated in the Olympics in 1992, when the U.S. team was known as the "Dream Team." The United States has won every gold medal since. In 1995, the NBA went international when the Toronto Raptors and Vancouver Grizzlies joined.

For his part in starting all this, James Naismith was honored in 1968 when the Naismith Memorial Basketball Hall of Fame was opened on the campus of Springfield College, the new name of the International Training School where he invented the game. The hall moved off campus in 1985 into a modern building and by 2003 had inducted 246 individuals and five teams into the Hall of Fame.

## THE RULES

A team has five players, who score points by tossing the ball through the basket—either by shooting field goals when the ball is in play or, after being fouled, by shooting extra points, known as foul shots. Two points are awarded for a field goal—or three if the shot is taken from beyond the three-point line, which is 23 feet 11 inches (7.25 m) facing the basket or 22 feet (6.70 m) from the sides.

Young players are the future stars of tomorrow's college and professional games. Teams exist for children as young as five, which proves you can score a basket without being 7 feet (2.13 m) tall.

# BOB PETTIT (1932–)

A forward with the St. Louis Hawks, Bob Pettit was the first NBA player to score 20,000 points, ending his career with 20,880 in 792 games. Amazingly, he was once cut from his high school team in Baton Rouge, Louisiana. However, urged by his father to practice on his backyard hoop, he later returned to the team and led it to the state championship.

A two-time All American at Louisiana State University, Pettit was considered too slightly built to survive the rough professional game. However, he began his career in 1954 with the Milwaukee Hawks, where he was the NBA Rookie of the Year, and followed the team when it moved to St. Louis, guiding it to the NBA championship in 1958.

In 1956 and 1959, Pettit led the NBA in scoring and was named Most Valuable Player twice. He also made the All-Star team eleven times. His 12,849 rebounds for a 16.2 average per game was a league record when he retired in 1965.

Bob Pettit played for LSU from 1950 to 1954. He was inducted into the Naismith Basketball Hall of Fame in 1970 and named in 1974 as the greatest player in Southeastern Conference history.

A successful free throw, or foul shot, equals one point and is taken from a line 15 feet (4.5 m) from the basket, after play is stopped.

Professional games last forty-eight minutes with twelve-minute quarters; college games are forty minutes divided into twenty-minute halves; high school games are thirty-two minutes with eight-minute quarters. If a game is tied at the end, five-minute overtimes are played until one team is ahead at the end of an overtime.

The size of the court varies, from 50 x 84 feet (15.2 x 25.6 m) for high schools, 50 x 90 feet (15.2 x 27.4 m) for colleges, and 50 x 94 feet (15.2 x 28.6 m) for professional teams, both men and women. Each goal is 10 feet (3 m) above the floor. The five players' positions are one center, two forwards, and two guards.

## Getting started

Games begin with one player from each team facing each other. The referee tosses up a "jump ball," and each player tries to tip it to his or her team. A player with the ball can "dribble" it by bouncing the ball on the floor with one hand. If he stops dribbling and holds the ball, he cannot dribble again but must pass or shoot. If he takes steps with the ball without dribbling, he is called for "traveling," and the other team gets the ball.

An offensive player may also pass or roll the ball to a teammate. The offense must take a shot within a certain number of seconds shown on the shot clock (twenty-four for the NBA, thirty-five for college men).

The defensive team can get the ball by intercepting passes, blocking shots, knocking it out of the ball carrier's hands, or catching a missed shot as it rebounds (comes down) off the backboard. If a basket is successfully made, the other side gets the ball. If a high school or college player commits five fouls, or six in the NBA, he must leave and not reenter the game.

# The Mental Game

**Mental attitude often makes the difference in the success of basketball players and their teams. Almost all NBA and WNBA players go through a mental routine before a game because a player's physical body is driven by the mind. And players on the court need confidence and mental toughness.**

Whether defending against a star shooter or standing alone on the free-throw line for a possible game-winning point, a player's ability lies partly in the mind. By controlling your thoughts to increase motivation, alertness, and concentration, you can create a winning attitude and also play a safer game.

Basketball players can actually increase their skills and success by forming a mental picture of playing well. Mental imagery, which is called **visualization**, is a proven method used by players in every sport. The great golfer Jack Nicklaus, for instance, said he always imagined the ball ending up in the cup even before he selected a club. "It's like a color movie," he said. "First, I 'see' the ball where I want it to finish, nice and white, and sitting up high on the bright green grass. Then the scene quickly changes, and I 'see' the ball going there: its path, trajectory, and shape, even its behavior on landing."

Like Nicklaus, a basketball player can learn to see success before it happens. You can create a vivid picture in your mind of many successful scenes: jumping high to make a perfect shot, stealing the ball and going the length of the court for a

The slam dunk is one of basketball's most exciting plays. It is not easy to throw the ball down into a basket that is 10-feet (3-m) high, but some players can do it backward and over the head.

**lay-up**, standing at the foul line and making two shots that swish through the net. You have probably made fine plays in previous games, so rehearse these in your mind, too, as if you were watching yourself on television.

The key to visualization is to make the image as realistic as possible, like Jack Nicklaus's "color movie." Imagine the entire atmosphere as you are on the court, with all the sounds of squeaking shoes, the smack of the ball on the floor, the shot clock ticking down, the referee's whistle, players calling to each other, the coach shouting directions, the sounds of the excited crowd, and your own breathing and concentration. Feel the ball on your fingers or the towel tossed to

The popularity of girls' and women's basketball teams continues to grow. The many college teams provide excellent players to the Women's National Basketball Association.

The basketball net was made out of wire in the late nineteenth century. That would make it hard to cut down the net, which is a school tradition after winning a championship game.

# WHAT PEOPLE SAY ABOUT BASKETBALL

**James Naismith, basketball inventor:**

*The invention of basketball was not an accident. It was developed to meet a need. Those boys simply would not play 'Drop the Handkerchief.'*

**Bill Vaughn, author:**

*Any American boy can be a basketball star if he grows up, up, up.*

**Michael Jordan, Chicago Bulls player:**

*Every time I step onto the court, if you're against me, you're trying to take something from me. I don't want the other team to win. I just do not want them to win.*

**Bobby Knight, former Indiana University coach:**

*You don't play against opponents. You play against the game of basketball.*

**Abe Lemons, Oklahoma City University coach:**

*There are only two plays:* Romeo and Juliet, *and put the darn ball in the basket.*

**Tom Tolbert, Orlando Magic player:**

*I look at the NBA as a football game without the helmet.*

you during a timeout. Be aware of your emotions as you handle the ball, and sense victory approaching. Know that everything you "see" will lead to a positive outcome.

Mental imagery should also include close-ups of your actions on the court. Break down the picture into smaller movements, focusing on your footwork, how you will position your arms for a field goal or free throw, the action of your body on defense, and the movement of your head as you call for a pass. If you have been previously injured, remember the actions that caused this injury, and visualize the right movements to avoid making another such mistake.

Former Atlanta Hawks coach Lenny Wilkens gives frantic signals to his players. Emotional coaches often draw technical fouls because of their behavior.

## MENTAL PRACTICE

Visualization must be practiced regularly and become an important part of your preparations for competition. Do it before a practice or game, or even at any other time, such as while taking a bath or before falling asleep. A fifteen-minute session will help to focus your mind on success. The more often you "see" yourself making great plays, the more this will seem the normal situation. You will create and keep a positive self-image, and this will build confidence and

# GAME TACTICS

Basketball is a game that moves at such a fast pace you may wonder how it is possible to plan and carry out tactics. At college and professional levels, much time is spent in pregame preparation: many hours are spent watching videos of opponents' earlier games to assess their offense and defense, and coaches will alter their team's strategy both before and during a game to take advantage of opponents' weaknesses. Other general strategies have also proven to work. These strategies include:

## OFFENSE

- Screening play—A player stands between her teammate who has the ball and a defender. This action is called a "screen" or "pick." The player doing the screening is generally taller than the shooter.
- Fast break—Used by fast teams, this usually begins when a player rebounds an opponent's shot. His teammates immediately sprint down court to receive his long pass over the defenders' heads.
- Give-and-go—One player passes the ball to a teammate and immediately cuts toward the basket to receive the ball back and shoot. This often works because the defender guarding the first player will relax when the ball is passed.

## DEFENSE

- Full court press—Defensive players come right up to guard the opposing team that is throwing the ball into play in the backcourt (which is the farthest away from the offense's own basket). This can disrupt the offense and even lead to interceptions of the throw-in.

- Intentional fouling—A team behind at a late stage of the game will often foul an offensive player just to stop the clock. It is best to foul a player with the ball who has a poor record making free shots.
- Timeout—In strategic terms, a timeout enables a team to break the momentum of an opponent on a successful run. A full 75-second timeout is sometimes just enough to cool down a hot offense.

Blocking a shot is a difficult play. Jermaine O'Neal of the Indiana Pacers and Shawn Bradley of the Dallas Mavericks each blocked 228 shots in the 2000–2001 season.

reduce anxiety. Negative thinking has been proven to cause poor play and injuries, so it is important to keep good control of your attitude and emotions and build a positive self-image.

You will be especially receptive to mental imagery when in a relaxed state. Find a quiet space, then assume a restful position in which you can close your eyes and be free from distractions. A partially relaxed condition can even be maintained during a game. This is called **relaxed attention**, and it means controlling your thoughts, emotions, and tension while playing. Notice how self-absorbed and calm many basketball players become when waiting for another player's foul shot. They are practicing relaxed attention. Despite the energy required for a game, a player who controls anxiety and anger can avoid mistakes and injuries.

Many aids are available to help players learn visualization and relaxation techniques. Sports psychologists, physicians, and other health professionals have produced commercial videos and written books and training manuals on this subject. Another way of practicing visualization at no cost is to watch the best college and professional players in action. You can put yourself in their place, imagining that it is not the player but you who are making those clever moves, and feeling your body carry out the action.

A close basketball game between equal teams will most often be won by the team with the best mental attitude. Coaches spend a good deal of time motivating their players, but seldom provide instruction on basic exercises of mental preparation, such as visualization. Often, players must exchange ideas among themselves on how to relax, build confidence, reduce stress, and avoid injuries. The important idea is that mental conditioning backs up physical training, and this is a winning combination on the basketball court.

# TYPES OF FOULS

Basketball games are often won or lost from the free-throw line or because a good player fouls out. Illegal actions are divided into technical or personal fouls. A technical foul involves bad behavior that is usually not physical. Coaches may be charged for overreacting, such as running onto the court or yelling at an official. Players may be charged for touching an official, using obscenities, or complaining about a call.

Personal fouls include:

- Charging—The player with the ball collides with a defensive player whose feet are already firmly planted on the spot.
- Blocking—The defender's feet are not firmly planted before the ball carrier collides with him.
- Handchecking—A defender touches an offensive player facing her.
- Holding—A player grabs an opponent's uniform to hinder movement.
- Flagrant foul—An action which is so rough that it could result in an injury.

Collisions usually mean fouls, and disputes about whether it was a charging or blocking offense.

# Fitness to Avoid Injury

**Basketball has always been a contact sport, but stronger and more aggressive players have made the game much more physical—although not dangerous enough to bring back cages. The possibility of injury is always present, so pregame warm-ups and a long-term conditioning program are essential to reduce the risk.**

The warm-up session before each game is a good rehearsal of basketball skills. Watching a warm-up, you will notice that players often begin very leisurely, stretching their arms, bouncing the ball, passing it around a circle of players, and taking several unhurried shots at the basket. The tempo then quickens, as players pass the ball as a "hot potato" to loosen their arms and help eye–hand coordination. They also practice rebounding, and line up to make running lay-ups. All this involves the key abilities demanded by basketball: accuracy, teamwork, and special bursts of energy.

Such moderate exercise also prepares a player's body for the considerable demands that this fast game makes on muscles and the respiratory system. Basketball does not have football's routine breaks in action or baseball's half-

Dennis Rodman stretches before a game. Stretching can seem boring at times, but it is an essential activity to prepare a basketball player's body for the speed and agility required by the game.

Magic Johnson, the Los Angeles Lakers star, shows that even the best have to warm up their muscles before a game. These stretches were done before a contest in Israel.

inning rests. If no fouls occur, basketball players must have the stamina to race back and forth on the court for long periods of time without a pause.

## WARM-UP AND PRECONDITIONING

A pregame workout of even fifteen minutes will stretch and warm the muscles, ligaments, and connective tissues, making them supple, so that a player's body is more flexible. Stretching should start with the neck and work downward to the shoulders, back, and legs. This "loosening up" will cut down on injuries on the court that might have been caused by stiffness, such as muscle **strains**, pulls, or tears. These brief

# NUTRITION

Good eating habits, or correct nutrition, are essential for good health. Eat light foods before games and avoid dairy products close to playing. Remember, too, that dehydration can lead to fatigue. Symptoms include muscle cramps, light-headedness or dizziness, and a loss of energy. During a game, make sure that you drink plenty of water or a sports drink which will replace lost fluids.

Here are some other simple points about nutrition to remember:

- About 60 percent of your daily food should contain complex carbohydrates, which provide fuel. Good sources are fruit, vegetables, bread, pasta, rice, and cereals.

- About 20 percent of your daily food should contain protein, which builds muscle. Good sources are lean meats, fish, legumes, cheese, milk, and nuts.

- No more than 20 percent of your daily food should contain fat, although this does provide energy. The best sources are nuts, margarine, and vegetable oil.

- Avoid junk food, which is high in calories, salt, and fat, as well as candy, desserts, and soft drinks, which provide inadequate nutrients.

exercises will also add more oxygen to your body's system by increasing the heart and respiratory rates. Any exercise that provides an increased oxygen intake is called **aerobic** and will produce positive benefits less than a minute after the exercise begins.

Although basketball players do pregame stretching exercises on the court, they will not use the hard floor to engage in basic **calisthenics** such as sit-ups, push-ups, running in place, jumping jacks, and knee-bends, as seen before football games. If they want to do such additional stretching and strength movements, they will use the dressing room.

After a game has ended, players should cool down for two to five minutes to help slow the heart and body to their normal tempo. The strenuous play on the

A basketball player's thighs are given special attention during warm-ups. This is Kentucky's Nazr Mohammed stretching his legs before a home game in Rupp Arena.

basketball court causes a player's heart to work hard to pump blood to the muscles, and blood that remains in the muscles causes a sore or stiff feeling after the game. Walking or stretching in the dressing room will relieve this, but sitting down immediately after an exhausting game could cause dizziness or fainting.

Equally important are programs that condition an athlete throughout the year. Aerobic and strength conditioning are the best ways to build up insurance against fatigue, which has been proven to cause more injuries on the court. Any combination of running, swimming, cycling, and warm-up exercises will be beneficial. A player's endurance and general good health will be improved by only three days a week of good strenuous exercise lasting for twenty to thirty minutes. Too much physical training, however, can cause exhaustion, stress, and poor performance. Young players, who are still growing, should not do heavy weight training, as this may damage the cartilage where growth occurs.

## EXERCISING TO BE FLEXIBLE

Upper body warm-up exercises concentrate on the neck, arms, shoulders, waist, and back:

- Stretch the neck by grabbing the back of the head with the right hand and pulling the head to the right. Repeat with the left hand.
- For the arms and shoulders, here are six exercises:
  1. Stretch the arms upward and backward.
  2. Reach the arms toward the sky one at a time.
  3. Rotate the arms forward in circles on either side, moving one up as the other descends.
  4. Hold each elbow behind the head in a pulling motion.
  5. Raise arms to shoulder level, pulling them back and holding the position.

6. Raise the shoulders while keeping the arms next to the body, then move the shoulders backward in slow circles and then forward.

- For the waist, hold the arms out to the side and swing them as you twist your body back and forth to the right and left.

- For the back, lie on your front with your legs crossed at the ankles and your arms straight out in front. Raise your upper body off the floor five times, holding each time for one second, then slowly lower it back to the floor.

Flexibility exercises for the lower body, so important in basketball, are usually done either sitting or lying down:

- For knees and ankles, lie down and move each knee in turn toward the chest five times.

- For the hips and **hamstring** muscles, sit with legs spread and knees locked, then bend forward to grasp each ankle in turn. Hold for ten seconds. Repeat five times for each ankle.

- For a second hamstring stretch, lie on your back with one leg straight out and one leg bent with the foot flat on the floor. Grab the back of the knee with both hands, and slowly pull the leg to your body as far as possible. Repeat with the other leg. Warm up your thighs by touching your toes ten times from either a standing or sitting position.

In this exercise for the back muscles, you lie on your stomach, raise your legs off the floor, and cross one leg over the other.

# CONDITIONING TIPS

1. Before any exercise session, always remember first to do a light warm-up and to stretch.

2. Begin your conditioning program by exercising lightly, from thirty minutes to an hour, depending on your fitness level. Slowly increase the time each day. It will take from six to eight weeks to reach top condition.

3. Do not exercise or practice basketball for more than ninety minutes each session. The key to conditioning is physical intensity and concentration, not longer workouts.

4. Select exercises for flexibility and strength, and add relaxation techniques.

5. Exercise to the full capacity of your body's limits, but never endanger your health or safety by going beyond them.

The leg extension exercise shown here utilizes a bench and a machine with a padded bar that you have to raise slowly with your legs.

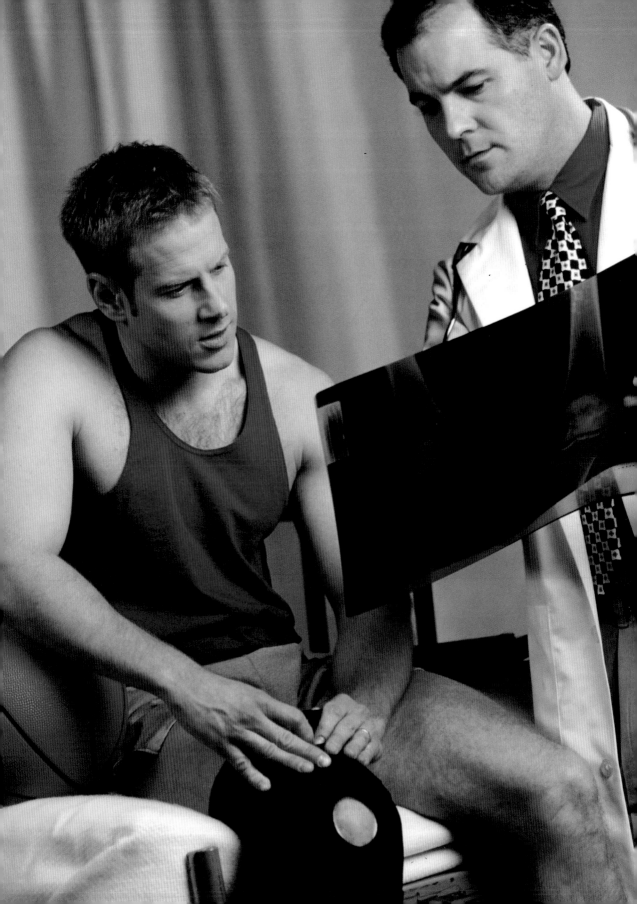

# Injuries and Treatment

**Basketball could certainly be played free of injuries. It is exciting enough as a game of skill, letting a player display fancy dribbling and footwork along with a precise aim. But the enthusiasm of competition and a lack of protective equipment means that there are many injuries each season.**

A survey by the U.S. Consumer Product Safety Commission of players aged five to fourteen found that basketball, surprisingly, led all sports in the annual number of injuries, with 574,000 incidents—more than double those of baseball and over 100,000 more than football.

There are very few protective items for basketball payers, but these can reduce injuries. A mouth guard will protect the mouth and teeth, and any player wearing glasses should switch to safety glasses. Knee and elbow pads offer good protection from bruises and **abrasions**, and ankle supports can be worn to reduce the chance of ankle **sprains**. The most important equipment, however, is a good pair of basketball shoes that offer support, fit snugly, and grip the floor tightly without skidding. This can reduce everything from ankle sprains to knee injuries and lower back pain. And shoes that are not the right size, or that have poor support around the feet and ankles, may cause blisters.

Doctors will often take X-rays and scans to determine if a player has suffered such serious injuries as a fracture, dislocated shoulder, or concussion.

A key factor with regard to injuries is the condition of the court. The goals must be adequately padded, and the walls behind them should also be padded and not too close to the basket. The boundary lines should not be near the officials' table, bleachers, or other structures. The floor must also be clean, without debris, and not slippery. If the game is played outside, the court area should be free of natural hazards, such as holes and rocks, and night games must be properly lit.

## TYPES OF INJURY

During a game, players should be alert to the danger of collisions, keeping an eye on other players' movements. Another way of reducing injuries is to play fair, refraining from tripping, pushing, holding, elbowing, blocking, and charging into opponents. Still, the following types of injury occur due to collisions, rough contact, and falls:

• **Acute, or acute traumatic, injury**
This can be caused by any hard hit during a game, such as a collision with another player or a bad fall. Acute injuries include **contusions**, abrasions, **lacerations**, sprains, strains, and **fractures**. "Contusion" is the medical name for a bruise, which may be bad enough to cause swelling and bleeding in the muscles or other tissues. An abrasion is a scrape, and a laceration is a cut that is usually deep enough to require stitches. A sprain is a stretch or tear of a ligament, which is the tissue that supports joints by connecting bones and **cartilage**. If a stretch or tear occurs in a muscle or **tendon**, this is a strain. A fracture involves a crack, break, or shattering of a bone.

• **Overuse, or chronic, injury**
This kind of injury is caused by repeating the same action many times, as when a center rebounds the ball and experiences an ache in her ankles or knees. This is

A basketball player's best "equipment" is a good pair of shoes. They are needed for quick turns, accelerations, and stops. Well-fitting shoes can also reduce injuries.

not as serious as an acute injury, but any chronic problem may become worse during the season, so players should seek medical advice and treatment.

## COMMON INJURIES

Basketball requires the active use of the whole body. The lower part is injured most often, but the upper body, including the head, can sustain injuries, particularly in a hard fall. Common injuries, categorized by areas of the body, are:

## LEG AND ANKLE

**Players have to sit out many basketball games because of injuries to the leg and ankle.**

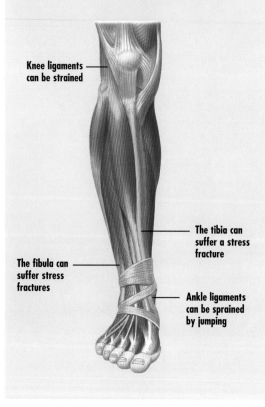

Knee ligaments can be strained

The tibia can suffer a stress fracture

The fibula can suffer stress fractures

Ankle ligaments can be sprained by jumping

## Ankle and foot

Because basketball is a game of running and jumping, it places great demands on your feet and ankles. The most common plays, such as quickly cutting around a defensive player or leaping high for a rebound, which may result in an uncertain landing, subject ankles and feet to continuous stress. Young players put additional wear and tear on these parts when they play on outdoor concrete courts. The strenuous action on any court can result in ankle sprains, heel bruises, and fractures.

A sprain that severely stretches the ligaments of the outside ankle is fairly common in basketball because players

# REHABILITATION (REHAB)

The recovery period after an injury may take several weeks or even months. Once the pain has subsided, you might feel completely fit, but follow your doctor's advice about changes to your athletic activity or even time away from the game.

Such injuries as sprained ankles and dislocated shoulders can quickly return if you reenter competition too soon. And even after rehabilitation, an injured area may begin to hurt again during a game. If so, stop immediately and tell your doctor.

Depending on how badly you are injured, your road back to fitness may include physical therapy or ultrasound to the injured area. Rehabilitation will also include an exercise program because an injury will cause you to lose strength. (If, for example, you wear a cast on your arm or leg for about six weeks, you may lose up to 40 percent of the strength you had in that arm or leg before the injury.) Recommended exercises may include swimming or workouts on gym equipment, such as a rowing machine.

make rapid changes in direction. You will feel immediate pain and sometimes hear a crack when a tear occurs. Any sprain will be followed by swelling, and a trainer or coach will apply ice to the ankle when the player returns to the bench.

As soon as possible, begin a treatment program known as **R.I.C.E.**, which stands for Rest, Ice, Compression, and Elevation. Put the ice in a plastic bag, lay a towel on the injured ankle, and put the ice on the towel. Never place ice directly on the

# FEMUR FRACTURE

**Fractures to the shaft of the femur are rare, but take many months to heal.**

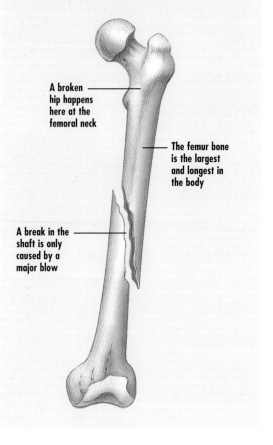

A broken hip happens here at the femoral neck

The femur bone is the largest and longest in the body

A break in the shaft is only caused by a major blow

injured area. Do this for about twenty minutes at a time, then repeat every two hours. Compression involves applying pressure to the ankle with an elastic bandage, making sure it is not tight enough to restrict circulation. Finally, elevate the ankle above heart level as much as possible. To provide support and prevent a recurrence of the injury, tape the ankle or use an ankle brace. A mild sprain should heal in about a week; severe ones can take up to six weeks.

A heel bruise can happen when a player leaps for the ball and lands incorrectly on the base of his heel instead of his toes. Poorly fitting shoes may also bruise the heels where the Achilles tendon attaches the back of the heel to the muscles of the calf of the leg. Achilles **tendonitis**, in which the tendon becomes inflamed, is a common injury. To treat heel bruises, follow the R.I.C.E. program and wear a doughnut-shaped felt pad on the bruised area.

A fracture to a foot bone is common when a player falls or when another competitor lands on her foot, especially during rebounds. A bone can also develop tiny cracks from overuse, such as the running and leaping required by the game, and this is

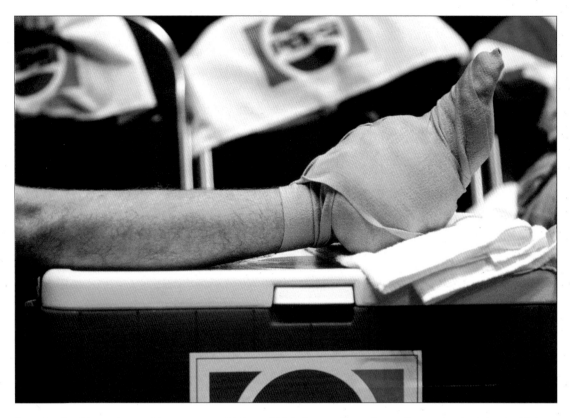

A sprained ankle receives quick treatment with ice, which helps to relieve the swelling and pain. It is part of the R.I.C.E. treatment of rest, ice, compression, and elevation.

called a **stress fracture**. Any fracture may hurt and cause a limp. The injured player should see a physician, who will take an X-ray. To heal a fracture, rest in particular is important, so follow the R.I.C.E. method and use a brace.

## Knee

Knee injuries are more serious than those of the ankle and foot. Many professional basketball players have suffered severe knee injuries that have shortened their careers. The game puts excessive tension on the knees and legs, especially when twisting the body while the feet are planted. Concrete or poor court surfaces increase the hard jamming of the knee bones. Quick turns, collisions, and falls cause sprains and strains of the knee, as well as cartilage injuries and dislocated kneecaps. Overuse can also put too much stress on the knees and cause tendonitis.

A knee sprain involves a painful ligament stretch or tear, which can cause a snapping or popping sound. This often happens to the anterior cruciate ligament (**A.C.L.**) inside the knee joint, a ligament that protects the knee from too much forward and backward movement. The National Collegiate Athletic Association (NCAA) has found that female basketball players aged fifteen to twenty-five years suffer this injury about two to four times more often than male players.

Use the R.I.C.E. treatment for the sprains, and a splint or even crutches if necessary. For a player who wants to continue on to college or professional basketball, surgery is often recommended to repair the A.C.L. Knee strains to muscles or tendons may produce similar symptoms to a sprain and might also show bruises. Strains, too, will respond to the R.I.C.E. program.

## Cartilage injuries

Cartilage injuries can happen when a player has a leg firmly on the court and the knee is twisted hard. The cartilage breaks off from the knee bone, causing swelling and pain. The knee will develop stiffness and popping sensations, and it might be difficult to extend the leg because the knee locks. Players who are still growing are more likely to suffer this injury. About one-third of these injuries will heal with rest, although it may also be necessary to wear a cast for several weeks. Usually, however, surgery is required in older teens and adults.

A hard blow, such as falling to the court, can cause a dislocated kneecap, or patella. This movable bone at the front of the knee is pushed sideways, causing swelling and much pain. A bulge can develop on the side of the knee, and walking may be

## KNEE INJURY

**A knee injury can be serious and often shortens a basketball player's career.**

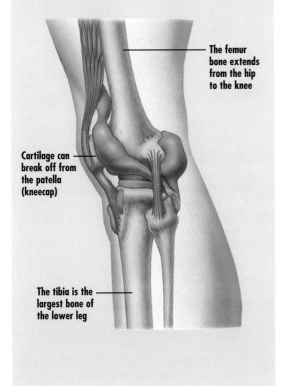

The femur bone extends from the hip to the knee

Cartilage can break off from the patella (kneecap)

The tibia is the largest bone of the lower leg

affected. Apart from the R.I.C.E. treatment, the kneecap may have to be reset by a physician, and the player may need to wear a brace to prevent a recurrence of the injury.

Tendonitis of the knee is an inflammation of a tendon, especially the one that connects the kneecap to the thigh bone. It is sometimes called "jumper's knee" and is an overuse injury caused by running and jumping, which stretches the tendon. This causes swelling and pain when walking, bending the knee, or trying to lift or extend the leg. Again, R.I.C.E. is the best treatment.

## Leg

Injuries to the leg are a fact of life in basketball, and they are frequently caused by players using their legs to jockey for position or by defensive players trying to block the progress of the ball handler. The injuries range from common contusions to hamstring pulls and infrequent fractures that are generally caused by falls. A leg contusion, or bruise, is a common injury, especially in the **quadriceps**. The soreness can be reduced by ice packs, and the bruise will soon go away. Deeper bruises, however, rupture blood vessels in the area, and this

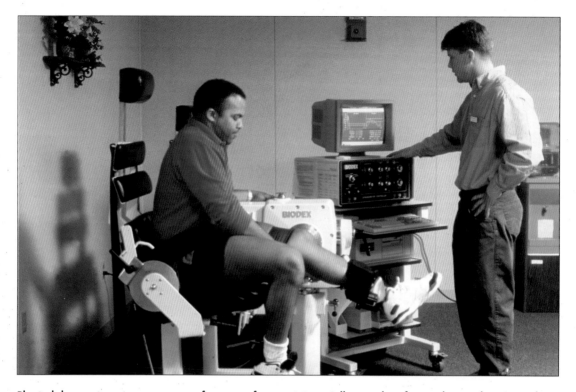

Physical therapy is an important part of recovery from an injury. College and professional teams have specialists to help with this part of rehabilitation, which may take weeks or months.

blood can collect and cause serious problems if the muscle continues to be exercised. The most important part of the R.I.C.E. program for this injury is to elevate the leg to reduce the blood pooling. A physician should also always be consulted in the case of deep bruises.

Hamstring pulls (strains or tears) involve the large hamstring muscles at the back of the thigh and are usually associated with running and jumping. The muscle fibers are strained when a player runs fast, then suddenly changes the motion of her thigh, from being pulled forward by the quadriceps to being pulled backward by the hamstrings. To treat, use R.I.C.E. along with stretching exercises, and take about a four-week rest from playing.

Fractures occur rarely in basketball, but broken legs (and arms) may result from a severe fall or violent collision with another player. More common are stress fractures due to overuse. Both types of fracture occur most often in the tibia (the larger leg bone below the knee) and fibula (the outer, thinner leg bone below the knee). Male players have more fractures of the tibia and females more of the fibula. A physician will take X-rays and then, depending on the seriousness of the injury, fit splints or recommend that the player use crutches.

## Hands, wrists, and fingers

Injuries to these areas occur while receiving passes, shooting, rebounding, and while breaking falls. Wrists are commonly sprained when the hand is bent too far forward or backward. The thumb and other fingers can be sprained, dislocated, jammed, or fractured when catching the ball or falling. Players can also develop regular and stress fractures in all of these bones. If the pain does not go away within twenty-four hours, consult a doctor. X-rays are needed, and treatment includes ice and, in the case of fractures, a splint.

## Shoulders

Shoulders can be injured by overuse, which causes strain, inflammation, or tendonitis. More severe are the two main injuries caused by falls and collisions: a shoulder separation or dislocation.

The separation of a shoulder involves a ligament tear that causes the collar bone to move upward. This is normally corrected by rest and strengthening exercises. A rehabilitation period is usually required before a player can return to the court.

A dislocated shoulder occurs when the head of the humerus (upper arm bone) pops out of its socket. This requires immediate treatment. The dislocation is

Falls are a main source of basketball injuries, because players wear little protective equipment. A forward fall such as this can cause injuries to the knees, hips, ribs, elbows, and hands.

generally caused by a torn cartilage or loose ligaments. X-rays will be taken, and a shoulder sling should be worn for about three weeks. The most serious dislocations require surgery.

## Neck

Serious neck injuries are rare in basketball. A more frequent problem is a "stinger" injury, which occurs when the nerves of the neck are overstretched, causing stinging pain and a temporary numbness. Pinched nerves, which can be caused by a quick sideways twist of the neck, produce a burning pain in both the neck and often down the arm. The standard treatment is the R.I.C.E. program.

Minor neck injuries, including bruises and sprains, may require that the player wear a neck collar or brace. Much more dangerous is a fracture to the spine: the vertebrae and discs can be compressed by a hard fall on the court when the head is bent forward. This injury is very rare, but a player lying still on the court should not be moved until qualified emergency personnel arrive because movement could cause paralysis or death. X-rays will reveal the extent of the injury.

## Head

Severe falls during play may also result in a concussion. This injury is normally mild, causing such problems as a headache, poor balance, a lack of alertness, memory loss, and sometimes unconsciousness. There is a very rare chance that such a blow can cause pressure and a hematoma (bleeding under the skull), which can be fatal. For this reason, a physician will order X-rays and scans to eliminate such a possibility. Any head injury will require a player to wait for at least a week, even a month, after the symptoms disappear before returning to competition.

Players can continue to play with minor injures, but they need protection to avoid reinjury, such as this Italian player's nose shield.

# Careers in Basketball

**Because basketball requires so little equipment and only five players for a team, most young people are very familiar with the game at the neighborhood level. Good basketball teams can be sponsored by small schools that could never afford a football program and by urban schools without the space for a stadium.**

Before high school, players have the option of joining a recreational youth team, such as those supported by the YMCA, the Boys & Girls Clubs of America, the National Police Athletic Leagues, the National Recreation and Parks Association, and the Jewish Community Centers of North America. More than 500,000 boys and girls, aged five to fourteen years, from the United States, Canada, and elsewhere participated during the 2001–2002 season in a network of about a thousand leagues. These are supported by the Jr. NBA/Jr. WNBA organization, which provides instructional materials, advice, and league promotion, and also organizes visits from NBA and WNBA stars. Annual tournaments also exist, such as those conducted by Youth Basketball of America. This is an international governing body that hosts both national and international championship tournaments for boys and girls.

High school basketball, which had 549,500 participants for the 2002–2003 season, is an ideal showcase for good players who wish to continue the sport at the college

If life is a game, then basketball is a very profitable one, especially if you are Michael Jordan, once listed as the best paid athlete in the world. Any NBA player can also make a good living.

level, and many such students apply for partial or full athletic scholarships. Star players will easily draw the attention of college scouts, and pro scouts will even court exceptional athletes. Several high school players have skipped college and gone directly into the professional game. Moses Malone, for example, signed with the Utah Stars of the American Basketball Association upon graduation from high school. Most players, however, seek the benefits of a college education and the spirited excitement of intercollegiate basketball.

## COLLEGE BASKETBALL

Colleges are beginning to recruit players who are not yet high school seniors. In 2001, the NCAA approved the recruitment of juniors who had finished their basketball season, saying they could visit prospective programs. Universities who have received commitments from juniors include the University of Arizona, Duke University, the University of Cincinnati, Gonzaga University, the University of Kentucky, Michigan State University, and Xavier University (of Cincinnati). Some schools are actively recruiting high school sophomores: In 2003, Texas Tech's coach Bobby Knight received a

Youth leagues give players fine training and many opportunities to compete. Annual championship tournaments are a highlight for youngsters.

# KAREEM ABDUL-JABBAR (1947– )

Born Lewis Alcindor in New York City, this athlete stands 7 feet 2 inches (2.18 m) and dominated the game. In high school, he led his team to seventy-one consecutive victories. He then powered UCLA to an 88–2 record and won three straight NCAA titles (1967–1969), developing his famous "skyhook." He is the only player in history to have been named the NCAA tournament's Most Outstanding Player three times.

In 1969, he joined the Milwaukee Bucks and was Rookie of the Year, averaging 28.8 points a game. He also became the league's Most Valuable Player a record six times, and still holds the NBA record for the most career points—38,387. Jabar was traded to Los Angeles Lakers in 1975, leading the team to five NBA championships (1980, 1982, 1985, 1987, and 1988). When he retired in 1989, he led nine NBA statistical categories. Among these were records for field goals made and attempted (15,837 of 28,307), and blocked shots (3,189).

After retiring, Kareem Abdul-Jabbar went on to coach the NBA's Los Angeles Clippers in 2000 and Indiana Pacers in 2002.

commitment from a sophomore who stands 6 feet 7 inches (2 m). Even top high school freshmen are being evaluated.

Winning a college basketball scholarship, and even a place on a team, is highly competitive. There were 15,700 college participants in the 2002–2003 season, which represents only 2.9 percent of those who played high school ball. To win a place on a college team, a high school player's best chance comes from having excellent performances on the court, no serious injuries, and good academic grades. Reliable high school players who are not stars will need to promote themselves to the colleges of their choice. Begin in your junior year by inquiring to your favorite colleges about basketball possibilities. Many colleges will send an

College basketball is played before loud, supportive home crowds, such as this game between the host team, Kentucky, and Tennessee.

interested player a recruitment questionnaire and form to fill out. They will ask for such information as the name of your high school coach and his or her contact number, your cumulative grade point average (GPA), S.A.T. scores, date of graduation, basketball statistics, and top three college choices.

If you have a strong ambition to play college ball, you can increase your chances by asking your high school coach to write or phone the coaching staff at your preferred schools. You can also influence college recruiters by mailing them clippings of your best performances or phoning to ask for a

Female students in the United States have played basketball since 1893. They now play the sport at all school levels, and college teams have regular seasons that lead to an NCAA Championship.

meeting on campus or even a tryout. The week-long signing period for high school players occurs in November. Few commitments happen from December through February, but then recruiting picks up again, with senior and junior candidates being invited to visit campuses in the spring. Full scholarships are not frequently awarded. The NCAA, for example, allows only the larger schools in its Division I-A to grant five scholarships for men's teams during any one year, and not more than eight in any two years.

Successful college and university teams appear often on national television and provide the best spotlights for talented players wishing to turn professional. The

# MICHAEL JORDAN (1963– )

How famous is Michael Jordan? Well, the ESPN television network named him "Athlete of the Century." He is the man who led the Chicago Bulls to six NBA championships; led the league in scoring for a record ten years, including seven straight seasons; and set an unbeaten record of 31.5 points a game. In 2002, he became only the fourth player in history to score more than 30,000 points. And he also won two Olympic gold medals with the "Dream Team" in 1984 and 1992.

Even more amazing is the fact that Jordan accomplished all this while battling injuries—broken ribs, back spasms, tendonitis in his wrist, and a torn cartilage in his knee. He missed sixty-four games in 1985 after breaking his foot and was out in 2002 for knee surgery.

Jordan retired in 1993 to play baseball, but returned to basketball two years later to lead the Bulls to a record seventy-two wins. He retired again in 1999, but came back in 2001 and ended his career with the Washington Wizards, retiring (finally?) in 2003 at the age of forty.

A poll of young people aged twelve to seventeen ranked Michael Jordan as their most admired athlete.

NBA has twenty-nine teams, which need a total of more than three hundred players. Professional scouts have the ability to pick out future superstars on any college team, but it helps a candidate's chances to be on a team that is a league champion and progresses well through the NCAA or NIT tournaments. Below are some of the most successful college programs.

## Men's Division I

University of Kentucky, University of North Carolina, University of Nevada at Las Vegas (UNLV), University of Kansas, University of California at Los Angeles (UCLA), St. John's University (New York), Duke University, Syracuse University, Western Kentucky University, University of Arkansas, University of Utah, Indiana University, Temple University, University of Louisville, University of Notre Dame, Purdue University, DePaul University, University of Illinois, Weber State University, University of Arizona, University of Pennsylvania, Villanova University

## Women's Division I

University of Tennessee, University of Notre Dame, University of Connecticut, Purdue University, University of North Carolina, Texas Tech University, Stanford University, Louisiana Tech University, Old Dominion University, University of Southern California, University of Texas, Auburn University, University of Georgia

## Men's Division II

Kentucky Wesleyan University, University of Evansville, University of North Alabama, Saint Michael's College, South Dakota State University, Southern Illinois University, California State University of Bakersfield, North Kentucky University, University of Southern Indiana

# BASKETBALL CODE OF CONDUCT

Rick Wolff, the Youth Sports Expert with the Jr. NBA/Jr. WNBA, has created a ten-point Player's Code of Conduct:

1. Remember the golden rule—Always treat everyone (whether teammate or opponent) how you would like to be treated.
2. Be a good sport—Play fair. Be a leader. Set the example.
3. Practice the fundamentals—Master the basketball basics.
4. Listen to your coach—That is part of the deal.
5. Be patient with teammates—Every player has both strengths and weaknesses.
6. Learn the rules—How can you "know the game" if you do not know the rules?
7. Never question an official—All they want is a fair and safe game.
8. Play hard—Coaches absolutely love players who try a little harder and jump a little higher.
9. Include your parents—Let them into your basketball world, but remind them that there are ups and downs, and your goal is to have fun.
10. Have fun—Win or lose, try to enjoy every moment on the court. If playing is not fun, something is wrong.

## Men's Division III

University of Wisconsin at Platteville, University of Wisconsin at Whitewater, Illinois Wesleyan University, University of Rochester, Potsdam State University, North Park University, Hope College

## GOING PROFESSIONAL

NBA teams draft college players in late June each year, and the system gives the first selections to the teams with the poorest records in the last season. Teams that did not make the playoffs participate in drawing table-tennis balls from a drum to determine which team can choose first, second, and so on.

Minor professional leagues also exist for players who do not make the NBA or WNBA, and these can provide a stepping stone to the top. The United States Basketball League has sent 130 of its players to the NBA, and it therefore calls itself "The League of Opportunity." Other minor leagues include the National Basketball Development League in the Southeast, the small Midwestern Basketball Association, the National Women's Basketball League with teams around the country, and the Women's American Basketball Association in the northeast.

Yolanda Griffith of the Sacramento Monarchs is one of the stars attracting fans to games of the Women's National Basketball Association (WNBA).

# Glossary

**Abrasion:** An injury caused when the top layers of skin are rubbed or scraped away.

**A.C.L.:** Abbreviation for the anterior cruciate ligament, found inside the knee joint.

**Aerobic:** Used to describe exercise that demands increased oxygen and so forces up the heart and breathing rates.

**Backcourt:** The defending team's half of the court.

**Calisthenics:** Exercises designed to improve suppleness and balance.

**Cartilage:** Strong connective tissue found in the body's joints and other structures. Children have a higher percentage of cartilage than adults. Some of this cartilage turns to bone as children grow older.

**Contusion:** The medical name for a bruise; the skin is not broken.

**Fracture:** A crack, break, or shattering of a bone.

**Hamstrings:** The group of three large muscles set at the back of the thigh.

**Laceration:** A cut that is deep enough to require stitches.

**Lay-up:** A jumping one-hand shot made from close under the basket.

**NBA:** Abbreviation for the National Basketball Association, which was established in 1949 when the National Basketball League merged with the Basketball Association of America.

**Physical therapy:** The treatment of an injury or illness using such physical techniques as massage and stretching, rather than medicine or surgery.

**Quadriceps:** A large four-part muscle on the front of the thigh, used to extend the leg.

**Relaxed attention:** A player's mental state of being partially relaxed during a game but still being attentive and able to control thoughts and emotions.

**R.I.C.E.:** An acronym for a common treatment program for nonserious injuries; it stands for "Rest, Ice, Compression, and Elevation."

**Sprain:** A stretch or tear of a ligament.

**Strain:** A stretch or tear of a muscle or tendon.

**Stress fracture:** A fracture caused by overuse of a bone.

**Tendonitis:** Inflammation and pain in tendons.

**Tendon:** A body tissue, also called a sinew, that connects muscles to bones.

**Ultrasound:** Sound waves that are outside the range of human hearing. Physical therapists sometimes use ultrasound machines to treat damaged muscles by sending the sound waves vibrating through the injured area.

**Visualization:** The technique of improving sports performance by imagining yourself playing well.

# Further Information

## USEFUL WEB SITES

For a history of basketball, see: www.all-sports-posters.com/
historyofbasketball.html

Basketball Hall of Fame: www.hoophall.com/halloffamers

National Basketball Association (NBA): www.nba.com

The Jr. NBA/Jr. WNBA: www.nba.com/jrnba

Women's National Basketball Association (WNBA): www.wnba.com

Youth Basketball of America: www.yboa.org

The Web sites listed on this page were active at the time of publication. The publisher is not responsible for Web sites that have changed their address or discontinued operation since the date of publication. The publisher will review and update the Web sites upon each reprint.

## FURTHER READING

Burgan, Michael. *Great Moments in Basketball.* Milwaukee: World Almanac Education, 2002.

Gutman, Bill. *Michael Jordan: Simply the Best.* Brookfield, Connecticut: Millbrook Press, 1995.

Mullin, Chris and Brian Coleman. *Basketball.* New York: Dorling Kindersley Pub Merchandise, 2000.

Roberts, Robin. *Sports Injuries.* Brookfield, Connecticut: Millbrook Press, 2001.

Weatherspoon, Teresa, with Tara Sullivan and Kelly Whiteside. *Teresa Weatherspoon's Basketball for Girls.* New York: John Wiley & Sons, 1999.

## THE AUTHOR

**Dr. John D. Wright** is a writer and journalist with many years of experience. He has been a reporter for *Time* and *People* magazines, a journalist for the U.S. Navy, and reported for newspapers in Alabama and Tennessee. He holds a Ph.D. degree in Communications from the University of Texas, and has taught journalism at colleges in Alabama and Virginia. He now lives in Herefordshire, England.

## THE CONSULTANTS

**Susan Saliba**, Ph.D., is a senior associate athletic trainer and a clinical instructor at the University of Virginia in Charlottesville, Virginia. A certified athletic trainer and licensed physical therapist, Dr. Saliba provides sports medicine care, including prevention, treatment, and rehabilitation for the varsity athletes at the University. Dr. Saliba holds dual appointments as an Assistant Professor in the Curry School of Education and the Department of Orthopaedic Surgery. She is a member of the National Athletic Trainers' Association's Educational Executive Committee and its Clinical Education Committee.

**Eric Small**, M.D., a Harvard-trained sports medicine physician, is a nationally recognized expert in the field of sports injuries, nutritional supplements, and weight management programs. He is author of *Kids & Sports* (2002) and is Assistant Clinical Professor of Pediatrics, Orthopedics, and Rehabilitation Medicine at Mount Sinai School of Medicine in New York. He is also Director of the Sports Medicine Center for Young Athletes at Blythedale Children's Hospital in Valhalla, New York. Dr. Small has served on the American Academy of Pediatrics Committee on Sports Medicine for the past six years, where he develops national policy regarding children's medical issues and sports.

# Index

Page numbers in *italics* refer to photographs and illustrations.

Abdul-Jabbar, Kareem *8*, 11, 53
ankle injuries 37, 40–2

basketball
    code of conduct 58
    history 9–14, 16
    international appeal 9, 10, 14
    rules 10, 12, 14, 17, 58
    tactics 24–5
Basketball Association of America
    (BAA) 14
baskets 9, 10, 17, *21*
Boston Celtics 14

cages 12
Chamberlain, Wilt 11
Chicago Bulls 22, 56
coaches 22, *23*, 24, 26, 27, 53, 54, 58
code of conduct 58
colleges 10, 11, 13, 16, 52, 54–5, 57–8
collisions 38 *see also* injuries
courts 12–13, 17, 38

dislocations *36*, 41, 44–5, 47–8
doctors *36*, 41, 43, 45, 47, 49

equipment
    baskets 9, 10, 17, *21*
    protective 37–8, *49*
exercises
    after injury 41, 47
    fitness 33, 35
    warm-up *28*, 29–30, 32, 33–5
    *see also* muscles; preparation

falls 38, *48 see also* injuries
flexibility 30, 33–4, 35
foot injuries 40, 42–3, 56
fouls *23*, 25, 27, 38
fractures *36*, 38, 42–3, 47

Golden State Warriors 14
Griffith, Yolanda *59*

hand and wrist injuries 47
Harlem Globetrotters 11, 13–14

head injuries *36*, 49

injuries
    ankle 37, 40–2
    dislocations *36*, 41, 44–5, 47–8
    feet 40, 42–3, 56
    fractures *36*, 38, 42–3, 47
    hand and wrist 47
    head *36*, 49
    knees 43–5, 56
    legs *42*, 45–7
    neck 48–9
    overuse 38, 40, 47
    rehabilitation 41, *46*
    R.I.C.E. treatment 41–3, 44, 45,
        46, 49
    shoulders 47–8
    sprains 37, 38, 40–2, 44, 47, 49

Johnson, Magic *30*
Jordan, Michael 22, *50*, 56

knee injuries 43–5, 56

leg injuries *42*, 45–7
Los Angeles Lakers 11, 53

mental preparation 19–20, 23, 26
muscles
    conditioning 33, 35
    hamstrings 34, 46
    stretching *28*, 30, 32–5
    *see also* exercises; injuries

Naismith, James 9–10, 14, 22
Naismith Memorial Basketball Hall of
    Fame *11*, 14
National Association of Intercollegiate
    Athletics (NCIA) 13
National Basketball Association (NBA)
    11, 16, 19, 51, 53, 56, 59
National Basketball League (NBL) 14
National Collegiate Athletic Association
    (NCAA) 13, 44, 52, 53, 55
neck injuries 48–9
New York Knickerbockers 14
Nicklaus, Jack 19–20
nutrition 31

Olympic Games 13, 14, 56

overuse injuries 38, 40, 47

Pettit, Bob 16
Philadelphia 76ers 11
Philadelphia Warriors 11, 14
physical preparation *28*, 29–35
physical therapy 41, *46*
positive thinking 19–20, 23, 26
preparation
    mental 19–20, 23, 26
    physical *28*, 29–35
    *see also* exercises
professional players 13–14, *50*, 59
protective equipment 37–8, *49*

Rest, Ice, Compression, and Elevation
    (R.I.C.E.) treatment 41–3, 44, 45,
    46, 49
Rodman, Dennis *28*
rules 10, 12, 14, 17, 58

scholarships 52, 54, 55
school basketball 13, 51–2, 54–5
shoes 37, *39*
shoulder injuries 47–8
sprains 37, 38, 40–2, 44, 47, 49
St. Louis Hawks 16
stretching *28*, 30, 32–5
surgery 44, 48

tactics 24–5
tendonitis 45, 47, 56

universities 10, 11, 13, 16, 52, 54–5,
    57–8

visualization 19–20, 23, 26

warming up *28*, 29–30, 32, 33–5
Women's National Basketball Association
    (WNBA) 13, 19, *20*, 51, 59

X-rays *36*, 43, 47, 48, 49

YMCA 9, 10, 12, 51